A Cup of Comfort

*Words to Soothe
Your Soul and
Warm Your Heart*

Emilie Barnes

with Anne Christian Buchanan

Paintings by Susan Rios

HARVEST HOUSE PUBLISHERS
Eugene, Oregon

A Cup of Comfort

Text Copyright © 2002 by Emilie Barnes and Anne Christian Buchanan
Published by Harvest House Publishers
Eugene, Oregon 97402

ISBN 0-7369-0769-6

For more information about other books and products available from Emilie
Barnes, please send a self-addressed, stamped envelope to:

> More Hours in My Day
> 2150 Whitestone Drive
> Riverside, CA 92506
> (909) 682-4714

Original artwork © Susan Rios. Licensed by Art Impressions, Canoga Park, CA.
For more information regarding artwork featured in this book, please contact:

> Art Impressions
> 9035-A Eton Avenue
> Canoga Park, CA 91304-1616
> (818) 700-8541

Text from this book previously appeared in *The Twelve Teas of Friendship* by Emilie
Barnes (Harvest House Publishers, 2001) and *A Cup of Hope* by Emilie Barnes
(Harvest House Publishers, 2000).

Design and production by Garborg Design Works, Minneapolis, Minnesota

Harvest House Publishers has made every effort to trace the ownership of all
poems and quotes. In the event of a question arising from the use of a poem or
quote, we regret any error made and will be pleased to make the necessary
correction in future editions of this book.

Unless otherwise indicated, Scripture quotations are taken from the Holy Bible,
New International Version®, Copyright © 1973, 1978, 1984 by the International
Bible Society. Used by permission of Zondervan Publishing House. Scripture quotations marked NASB are from the New American Standard Bible®, ©1960, 1962,
1971, 1972, 1973, 1975, 1977 by The Lockman Foundation. Used by permission.

Printed in Hong Kong

02 03 04 05 06 07 08 09 10 11 /NG/ 10 9 8 7 6 5 4 3 2 1

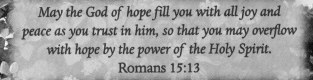

May the God of hope fill you with all joy and peace as you trust in him, so that you may overflow with hope by the power of the Holy Spirit.
Romans 15:13

*C*omfort can be found in a variety of things—food, family, memories, friends—but I continue to receive the most comfort from our heavenly Father as I journey through the Scriptures. I always enjoy sharing these moments of solace and blessed assurance with some of my closest friends. That's why I've chosen this gathering as one of my favorites because it's a delicate blend of friendship and comfort. So gather together those girlfriends who are near and dear to your heart for a wonderful time of caring, comfort, and cup of tea.

Emilie

*She could not speak, but she did "hold on,"
and the warm grasp of the friendly human
hand comforted her sore heart, and seemed
to lead her nearer to the Divine arm which alone
could uphold her in her trouble.*

LOUISA MAY ALCOTT

A Hearts-and-Hands Tea

It's wonderful to have friends when life is good, when we're happy and productive and confident. But it's when heartache strikes—when we face an illness or a loss or a disappointment—that we most deeply appreciate the bounty of true friendship. What an encouragement to have friends who will gather round in times of need, offering the gift of caring hearts and helping hands. And what a joy to be able to offer that gift of your heart and your hand to a hurting friend.

This teatime gathering is just one way you can offer the gift of loving support to a friend who is struggling. It's an offering of heart and hope that will lift the spirits of all who attend and will send the guest of honor away with the fortifying knowledge that she is truly loved.

I'll never forget a luncheon I threw years ago for a friend who was fighting cancer and about to undergo a bone marrow transplant. A small group of us gathered with her in my home to show our support. After a simple meal in the

Other refuge have I none;
Hangs my helpless soul on Thee;
Leave, O leave me not alone,
Still support and comfort me:
All my trust on Thee is stayed,
All my help from Thee I bring;
Cover my defenseless head
With the shadow of Thy wing.

CHARLES WESLEY
"Jesus, Lover of My Soul"

dining room, we moved into another room, where I had set out crayons, markers, rubber stamps, and all manner of craft supplies. I handed our guest of honor a stack of heavy paper and instructed her to trace her hand onto each sheet—one sheet for each guest. The handprints were passed around the table, and each woman drew a freehand heart in the center of "her" handprint. Then we all had fun decorating our sheets with crayons and markers—it was a little like being back in kindergarten again.

But coloring was not really what this party was about. The real purpose was our promise of ongoing love and prayer. For when we finished our handprints, we gathered together in a circle. Each of us put our hands on the hand of our sick friend and prayed for her. We hugged her and held her close. (We all cried together a little.) Then each of us took our decorated copy of her handprint home to post on our refrigerators—as a reminder to keep on praying.

What a poignant thing it was for me so many years later to be facing my own bone marrow transplant and to experience the same kind of loving support from my friends. During the months when I was waiting for the procedure, so many people held my hand over a cup of tea and prayed with me and hugged me. So many people symbolically placed their hands on mine as they placed my own handprint on their fridges.

I've come to believe that the loving support of people who care is one of the truest miracles we are given in our lifetimes. That means that when we use our caring and our imaginations to reach out to our friends, we are taking advantage of one of life's most precious opportunities—the chance to be part of a miracle. That's exactly what can happen at a gathering such as a hearts-and-hands tea.

Of all the heavenly gifts that mortal men commend,
What trusty treasure in the world can
   countervail a friend?

NICHOLAS GRIMALD

A Cup of Hope

*H*istory is full of stories of people who somehow managed to hold on to a stubborn hope long after they had stopped feeling hopeful, even after their conscious minds had stopped functioning well.

I think of Beck Weathers, the Texas physician who almost died during an expedition to Mt. Everest. Lost in a blizzard that killed the leader of his expedition, twice left for dead by his fellow climbers, Dr. Weathers somehow managed to get to his feet and stumble back down the mountain into camp. Some kind of hope buried deep inside him kept him putting one foot in front of the other.

Our life is like a tapestry of intricate design
With lovely patterns taking shape as colors intertwine,
Some of the threads we weave ourselves
By things we choose to do—
Sometimes a loving Father's touch adds a special hue.
And though tomorrow's pattern is not for us to see—
We can trust his faithful hand through all eternity.

AUTHOR UNKNOWN

A Comforting Setting

For a dash of colorful cheer, visit your grocery store or florist for pots of hopeful hyacinths in bright pink, lavender, and white. (Don't you just love their fragrance?) Or choose other bright and cheery flowers that happen to be in season. Cover the pots with swatches of print fabric in colors that coordinate with the blooms: just cut the fabric with pinking shears, fold up around the pots, secure with rubber bands, and hide the bands with festive ribbon bows. Cluster them in the middle of a table draped with a solid pink or lavender cloth. Continue the theme around the house as well. Line up a few small pots on a windowsill, for instance, and be sure to place arrangements in other rooms the guests will visit. If you'd like to use the "heart-in-hand" activity described above, you can create a pretty but useful activity area by covering card tables with the same fabric you used to cover the pots.

Don't forget the bathroom when you're decorating your home for tea—it's the one place that everyone is bound to visit. Spiff up that room with fingertip towels that match your tea table and a few more pots of the hyacinths. For a subtle touch, create a

> *Praise be to the God and Father of our Lord Jesus Christ, the Father of compassion and the God of all comfort, who comforts us in all our troubles, so that we can comfort those in any trouble with the comfort we ourselves have received from God.*
>
> THE BOOK OF
> 2 CORINTHIANS

By friendship you mean the greatest love, the greatest usefulness, the most open communication, the noblest sufferings, the severest truth, the heartiest counsel, and the greatest union of minds of which brave men and women are capable.

JEREMY TAYLOR

simple graphic of a hand with a heart on it on a sheet of paper, color it, and slip it into an inexpensive frame to hang in the bathroom.

If you have china with a pretty floral pattern, now is the time to use it. Simple white or clear glass will also work, especially if you hem squares of the print fabric for generously sized napkins and fluff them into the teacups or pull them through some pretty napkin rings.

A Cup of Hope

$\mathcal{I}$'m still on the mountain, so I've got to remember that my perspective is faulty. I just don't have the whole picture the way God does, the way I will have it someday.

Oh, I have some pretty good hints. I have instructions from the One who created the

mountain. I have stories from climbers who
have gone on the path before me and companions who have gone on the path before me and
companions who are climbing with me. (How
I depend on their help and encouragement!)
And of course I have those moments along the

way when wonderful
vistas suddenly unfold
before me, when I
round a corner to see
the checkered valleys
spread out below and
the summit shining
whitely up above.

I have all that to
enable me as I climb
up this mountain
called Life. You do,
too. I really believe
that the God who
created us and
redeemed us has
equipped us with
what we need to
make it to the top.

Become an answer to someone else's prayer.
Visit a sick relative or friend, call someone
and encourage them, mow a neighbor's yard,
give your spouse a back rub, write a check for
a local charity, compliment a coworker,
volunteer at a shelter for the homeless. Lift
your spirits by lifting someone else's load.

TRACY MULLINS AND ANN SPANGLER

Teatime Treats

Menu Suggestions:

    Heart-in-Hand Cookies

    Jasmine Spice Tea

    Golden Curry Chicken Salad Sandwiches

    Chocolate Chip Brownies

HEART-IN-HAND COOKIES

These are simple sugar cookies cut into the heart-and-hand shape and decorated beautifully. If you can't find a hand-shaped cookie cutter, you can trace a child's hand and make a cardboard template—or just cut small hearts out of large circles. This recipe will make about 3 dozen cookies, depending on the size of your cutters.

    2 cups butter, softened

    1½ cups sugar

    4 egg yolks

    2 teaspoons vanilla

    4½ cups unbleached flour

    ½ teaspoon salt

    1 tablespoon cinnamon

    1 hand-shaped cookie cutter about 3 inches long
        and at least 2 inches wide

    1 small heart-shaped cutter about 1 inch across

ROYAL ICING

　　2 teaspoons powdered egg whites (meringue
　　　　powder)
　　2⅔ cups confectioners' sugar
　　¼ cup water
　　red and blue food coloring

Preheat oven to 350°. Cream butter and sugar together in a mixer. Add egg yolks and vanilla. Mix well. Sift together flour, salt, and cinnamon. Beat into butter mixture. Chill dough about 1 hour. Roll out dough ¼-inch thick on lightly floured board. Use the hand-shaped cutter to cut out hand-shaped cookies and the heart-shaped cutter to cut a small heart out of the center. Gather scraps (including cutout hearts) and re-roll dough as needed. Place cookies on ungreased baking sheets and bake 12-14 minutes. Remove immediately and cool.

Blessed are they who have the gift of making friends, for it is one of God's best gifts. It involves many things, but above all, the power of going out of one's self, and appreciating whatever is noble and loving in another.

THOMAS HUGHES

For icing, combine all ingredients (except food coloring) and beat with an electric mixer for 8 to 10 minutes, until peaks form and icing is the texture of sour cream. Thin icing with water a drop at a time until about consistency of honey. Tint either pink or lavender with food coloring and spread on cooled cookies. Allow icing to harden before serving or storing.

GOLDEN CURRY CHICKEN SALAD SANDWICHES

The cashew nuts and raisins give these classic sandwiches a different twist. The recipe makes about 30 to 32 finger sandwiches.

> 2 cups very finely chopped chicken breast
> ½ cup each mayonnaise and sour cream
> ½ cup chopped celery
> ½ cup chopped cashew nuts
> ½ cup dried cherries or raisins
> ½ cup scallions, chopped with plenty of green
> 2 teaspoons curry powder
> nonstick cooking spray or a little canola oil
> 1 tablespoon lemon juice
> salt and pepper to taste
> dash of bottled hot sauce (optional)
> 1 loaf of light wheat bread
> unsalted butter, softened

In a large bowl, mix chicken, celery, cashews, and scallions. In a smaller bowl, mix mayonnaise and sour cream. Heat cooking spray or oil over medium heat in a nonstick skillet. Add curry powder and stir until

Friendship, peculiar boon of Heav'n,
The noble mind's delight and pride,
To men and angels only giv'n...

SAMUEL JOHNSON

blended. With a rubber scraper, scrape warmed curry powder into the mayonnaise/sour cream mixture. Add lemon juice and mix thoroughly. Stir this curry dressing into chicken mixture and mix well. Add salt, white pepper, and hot sauce to taste. To make sandwiches, spread slices of bread with unsalted butter. Spread filling between two slices of buttered bread (buttered side in). With a serrated knife, cut off crusts and then cut sandwiches into triangles to serve.

God stirs up our comfortable nests, and pushes us over the edge of them, and we are forced to use our wings to save ourselves from fatal falling. Read your trials in this light, and see if your wings are being developed.

HANNAH WHITALL SMITH

Craft Project

These easy-to-make candleholders are a beautiful tea table decoration, and they also make wonderful gifts for your treasured friends. Use clear glass votive candleholders—either straight-sided or rounded—and those little glass stones from the hobby store that are flat on one side. (They're often sold in the floral department to put in vases.) Look for a variety of warm, jeweled tones to cover either clear or colored votives. The only other tool you'll need is a glue gun and glue sticks, besides small candles to burn inside the cups.

To make the votives, begin by washing and drying

May your unfailing love be my comfort,
   according to your promise to your servant.
Let your compassion come to me that I may live,
   for your law is my delight.

THE BOOK OF PSALMS

your votive cup to remove the price tags and any accumulated dust. Heat up the glue gun, then glue a row of glass stones around the bottom of the votive cup. Continue to add glass stones around the bottom of the votive cup. Then add glass stones in rows up the side of the holder, varying the colors and staggering the stones from row to row, until you reach the top.

A true friend is the gift of God, and he only who made hearts can unite them.

ROBERT SOUTH

The rows of stones should be irregular and interlocked, but try to align those on the top row with edge of the glass. Let the glue harden, add a candle, and your jeweled votive is ready to grace your table!

If you like the effect of these jeweled candleholders, experiment with different colors of glass and even with other materials. Beach glass, marbles, bits of tile, and pieces of broken costume jewelry could all add texture and variety— or a simple, one-color scheme could decorate almost any space.

Having a friend is one of the greatest gifts you've ever had. Cherish it and invest in it.

The Twenty-Third Psalm (NASB)

The LORD is my shepherd, I shall not want.
He makes me lie down in green pastures;
He leads me beside quiet waters.
He restores my soul; He guides me in the paths
of righteousness for His name's sake.
Even though I walk through the valley of the
shadow of death,
I fear no evil; for Thou art with me;
Thy rod and Thy staff, they comfort me.
Thou dost prepare a table before me in the
presence of my enemies;
Thou hast anointed my head with oil; My cup
overflows.
Surely goodness and lovingkindness will follow
me all the days of my life,
And I will dwell in the house of the LORD forever.

I think that sometimes we miss out on the hope that God has for us because we insist on finding it where we want to find it—in the form that we want to find it—instead of opening our minds and our hearts to receive it as God wants to give it.

of Hope

Maybe we consciously set our hearts and our hopes on a happy, fruitful marriage...or a child...or a successful career...or an interesting life in a certain geographical area. Or maybe we just assume that our life will include certain amenities like good health or a happy family or a comfortable income. Then, if those wishes and assumptions are not fulfilled, we may find ourselves feeling disappointed and discouraged and even abandoned by God instead of joyful and hopeful and rejoicing in his presence.

We've gotten our hopes up, and we feel let down because life hasn't turned out the way we wanted. And as we mope about with our eyes cast down, we may find it hard to grasp the signs of new hope that are all around us.

How easy it is to miss out on hope when we forget who's in charge of the universe— and in charge of all we can hope for!

The Art of Helping a Friend in Need

*F*riends help friends—it's almost a definition of friendship. When any of us needs a loving heart or a helping hand, it's our friends we turn to, and the very acts of loving and helping in turn help cement our friendships. In fact, the relationships that last and grow over the years are often the ones that have been tested in the crucible of need. We all want to be that kind of friend to our chosen sisters, especially when they face hard times. Here are just a few specific ideas for how we can be truly helpful to a friend in need:

- *Be there.* If you can, offer your physical presence and your practical help. Volunteer to answer the doorbell, make phone calls, do the laundry, or grocery shopping, or sit by a bedside.

- *Pray for your friend on a regular basis.* Write it down on your to-do list. Don't underestimate

When comforts are declining,
He grants the soul again
A season of clear shining,
To cheer it after rain.

WILLIAM COWPER

I heard the voice of Jesus say, "Come unto
   Me and rest:
Lay down, thou weary one, lay down Thy
   head upon My breast."
I came to Jesus as I was, weary, and worn, and sad;
I found in Him a resting place, and He has
   made me glad.

HORATIUS BONAR
"I Heard the Voice of Jesus Say"

the power of prayerful support.

- *Speak carefully*. It's easy to let thoughtless remarks slip out, and people in times of difficulty can be especially sensitive.

- *Listen, listen, listen*. Then listen some more...even when you've heard it all a million times. Don't put a timetable on your hurting friend's recovery.

- *Don't let your friend push you away*. If she lashes out in anger toward her situation, you may become a target—just because you're there. Try to be extra tolerant and forgiving.

- *Be creative*. Carefully consider how you can use your mind, your heart, your imagination, your gifts and talents most effectively to help your friend. Your bookkeeping skills may be more helpful than your cooking, your gardening expertise more appropriate than your organizational skills.

- *Let love be your motivator*. Consider the idea that love sometimes takes us places we thought we'd never go. Even people who "don't do hospitals" may find themselves by the bedside of those they truly care about.

- *Offer long-term support.* Even when a crisis is past, healing may take a while. Make a point of asking your friend from time to time how things are going and how she's feeling. Write little notes of support from time to time. Remind her of all she has to offer and that things will get better. Keep offering the gift of your hands and your heart.

- *Lean on a community of love.* Work together with other people who love your friend—her family, other friends, her

Lord, dismiss us with thy blessing,
Hope, and comfort from above;
Let us each, thy peace possessing,
Triumph in redeeming love.

AUTHOR UNKNOWN

Peace is always beautiful.
WALT WHITMAN

church. In this way, you'll all support her
better, and you'll support each other as well.

• *Remember to let your friend help you, too.* When you
trust your friends with your needs and allow
them to care for you, you are giving them a tan-
gible gift of love. As your friend continues to
heal from her time of need, consciously give her
this gift by asking for her help and her prayers.

The hope He brings is always enough.